People of the Bible

The Bible through stories and pictures

David and Goliath

Copyright © in this format Belitha Press Ltd, 1985

Text copyright © Catherine Storr 1985

Illustrations copyright © Chris Molan 1985

Art Director: Treld Bicknell

First published in Great Britain in paperback 1985
by Methuen Children's Books Ltd,
11 New Fetter Lane, London EC4P 4EE

 Conceived, designed and produced by Belitha Press Ltd,
2 Beresford Terrace, London N5 2DH

ISBN 0 416 49220 7

Printed in Hong Kong
by South China Printing Co.

David and Goliath

Retold by Catherine Storr

Pictures by Chris Molan

Methuen Children's Books
in association with Belitha Press Ltd

One day, God spoke to Samuel, the High Priest.
He said, 'Saul, the King of Israel,
does not obey my commandments.
I am going to choose another king
to rule instead of him.

Go on a journey into the country.
Near Bethlehem you will find a man called Jesse.
I have chosen the new king from among his sons.'
Samuel said, 'Lord God, how can I do this?
If Saul hears of my journey, he will kill me.'

God said, 'Take an animal with you
and tell people that you are going to sacrifice to the Lord.'
The next day, Samuel journeyed towards Bethlehem.
When the people from the town saw him,
they were troubled.
They asked, 'Do you come in peace?'
Samuel said, 'I come in peace,
to make a sacrifice to the Lord.'

He called Jesse and his sons to the sacrifice.
When he saw Eliab, the eldest, he said,
'This must be the man I have come to find.'
But God said, 'No.
This is not the right man.'

Next, Samuel saw Abinadat,
but he was not the man God had chosen.
Then Jesse brought another son, Shammah,
and all the sons in his house for Samuel to see,
but not one was the right one.

Samuel asked, 'Have you no more sons?'
Jesse said, 'There is one more, the youngest,
He is out on the hills tending the sheep.'
Samuel said, 'Send for him.'

Jesse sent up to the hills,
and David, his youngest son, came down.
He was young and handsome to look at.
When Samuel saw him, he knew
that this was the boy God had chosen.
He took a horn of oil and annointed David
as the man who would one day be King of Israel.

It happened that at this time
Saul was troubled by an evil spirit.
He became very sad and miserable,
and he could not sleep.
His servants said, 'A cunning player on the harp
would drive away this evil spirit,
and you would feel better.'
Saul said, 'Very well. Find me such a man.'
A servant said, 'One of Jesse's sons
plays the harp, and he is very brave
and very good looking.'

Saul sent messengers to Jesse
To ask that David should come down to him.
When Jesse heard the message,
He sent bread and wine and a kid with David
As gifts for King Saul.
As soon as Saul saw David, he loved him.
David played the harp,
and his music calmed Saul
and the evil spirit left him.

A great war was being fought
between the Israelites and the Philistines.
The two armies were encamped on two mountains
on the opposite sides of a valley.
One of the Philistines was a giant called Goliath.
He was very tall and immensely strong.

He wore armour of brass
and his spear was as thick as a young tree.
He called out to the Israelites,
'Send out a man to fight me in single combat!'
But the Israelites were afraid.
No one would go out to fight Goliath.

Jesse's three eldest sons were in the army,
fighting with Saul against the Philistines.
One day, Jesse said to David,
'Take this measure of corn and these ten loaves.

Go to the camp and give these cheeses to the captain.
Find out how your brothers are.'
Early the next morning David went to the camp.
He heard Goliath shouting across the valley,
and he asked his brothers,
'What reward is there for the man
who will go out to fight this roaring giant?'

David's eldest brother was angry, and said,
'Why didn't you stay in the hills with your sheep?'
You just came down here to see the battle.'
David asked other people about Goliath.
Saul heard that a young man
was saying that someone should fight Goliath.
He sent for David, and David said to him,
'I will go out and fight this Philistine.'

Saul said, 'You can't fight Goliath.
He has been fighting for years
and you are only a boy.'

David said, 'For a long time
I have been guarding my father's sheep.'
Once a lion took a lamb,
but I made him drop it out of his mouth.
Then I took him by the beard and killed him.
I know that I can kill this Philistine
who is defying the army of the living God.'

When he heard that, Saul said,
'Go then, and God go with you.'
He gave David his own armour,
a brass helmet, a coat of mail and a sword.
But David said, 'I have never fought in armour,
I think I would do better without it.'

He took it off,
and went to the battlefield to meet Goliath.

As soon as Goliath saw the young David, he said,
'Am I a dog, that you come to fight me
without a sword, with only sticks?

Come nearer, and I will kill you,
and feed your body to the fowls of the air
and to the beasts of the field.'
David said, 'You come to fight me
with a sword and a spear,
but I come in the name of the Lord God.'
Then he put a stone into a sling
and hurled it at Goliath.
It hit the Philistine on the forehead,
so that he fell on his face on the earth.

David ran up and
stood on Goliath's body.
He took Goliath's sword
and cut off the giant's head.
Then the Israelite army
stood up and shouted,
and chased the Philistine army
up the valley
as far as the gates of Ekron.

After the battle, Abner, the Israelite captain,
brought David before Saul in Jerusalem.
David had with him Goliath's head and his armour.
Saul asked David, 'Whose son are you, young man?'
David said, 'I am the son of Jesse of Bethlehem.'
One of Saul's sons, called Jonathan,
Saw how handsome and brave David was.
He knew then that he would love this young man
as if he were his brother.

After this, David came to live
in the King's palace,
and he loved Jonathan too.

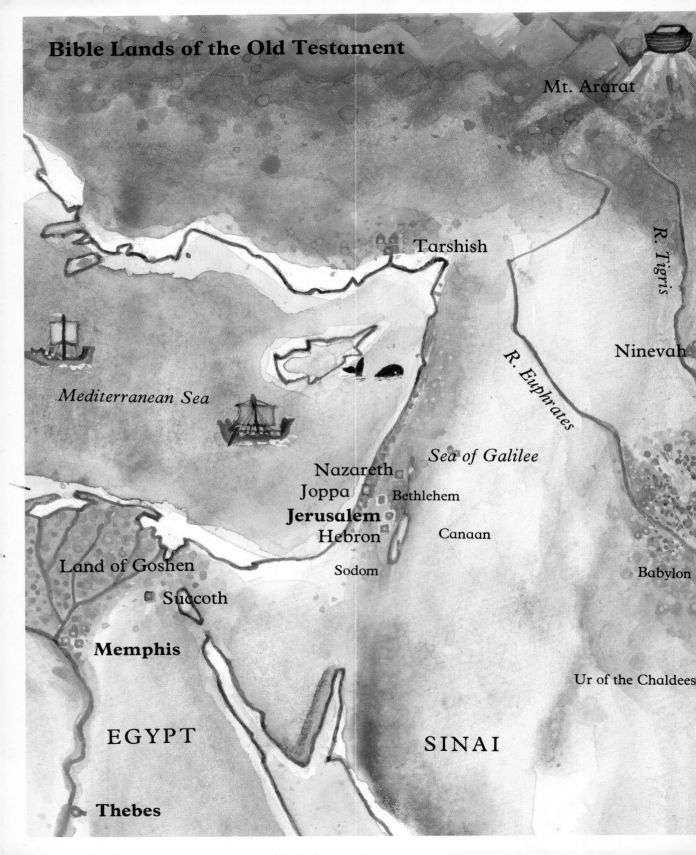

Bible Lands of the Old Testament

Mt. Ararat

R. Tigris

Tarshish

Ninevah

R. Euphrates

Mediterranean Sea

Sea of Galilee

Nazareth

Joppa   Bethlehem

Jerusalem

Hebron   Canaan

Sodom

Babylon

Land of Goshen

Succoth

Ur of the Chaldees

Memphis

EGYPT   SINAI

Thebes